BADLANDS
NATIONAL PARK
ACTIVITY BOOK

PUZZLES, MAZES, GAMES, AND MORE ABOUT BADLANDS NATIONAL PARK

NATIONAL PARKS ACTIVITIES SERIES

BADLANDS
NATIONAL PARK
ACTIVITY BOOK

Copyright 2021
Published by Little Bison Press

The author acknowledges that the land on which Badlands National Park is located are the traditional lands of Cheyenne, Mnicoujou and Očhéthi Šakówiŋ Tribes.

LITTLE BISON
Press

For more free national parks activities, visit
Littlebisonpress.com

About Badlands National Park

Badlands National Park is located in the state of South Dakota. Before it was a National Park, the Lakota people called this area "mako sica", which translates to "land bad". This is likely due to the challenging terrain and weather patterns that make traveling through very difficult.

The rugged beauty of the Badlands draws visitors from all over the world. It is home to striking geologic deposits that make up one the world's richest fossil beds. In fact, Badlands National Park area represents about 75 million years of Earth's history!

Visitors can visit the Sage Creek Rim Road or one of the many overlooks to best spot wildlife like bison, bighorn sheep, black-footed ferrets, and prairie dogs.

Badlands National Park is **famous for:**
- rock formations
- 244,000 acres of mixed-grass prairie lands
- fossil hunting
- many endangered species

Hey! I'm Parker!

I'm the only snail in history to visit every National Park in the United States! Come join me on my adventures in Badlands National Park.

Throughout this book, we will learn about the history of the park, the animals and plants that live here, and things to do here if you ever get to visit in person. This book is also full of games and activities!

Last but not least, I am hidden 9 times on different pages. See how many times you can find me. This page doesn't count!

Badlands Bingo

Let's play bingo! Cross off each box that you are able to during your visit to the national park. Try to get a bingo down, across, or diagonally. If you can't visit the park, use the bingo board to plan your perfect trip.

Pick out some activities that you would want to do during your visit. What would you do first? How long would you spend there? What animals would you try to see?

SPOT A BISON	SEARCH FOR A FOSSIL	IDENTIFY A TREE	TAKE A PICTURE AT AN OVERLOOK	WATCH A MOVIE AT THE VISITORS CENTER
GO FOR A HIKE	LEARN ABOUT THE INDIGENOUS PEOPLE THAT LIVE IN THIS AREA	WITNESS A SUNRISE OR SUNSET	OBSERVE THE NIGHT SKIES	GO STARGAZING
HEAR A BIRD CALL	SPOT A PRIARIE DOG	FREE SPACE	BECOME A BADLANDS JUNIOR RANGER	VISIT A RANGER STATION
PICK UP TEN PIECES OF TRASH	GO CAMPING	SEE A PRONGHORN	VISIT BADLANDS WALL	SPOT A BIRD OF PREY
LEARN ABOUT THE GEOLOGY OF THE BADLANDS	SEE SOMEONE RIDING A HORSE	HAVE A PICNIC	SPOT SOME ANIMAL TRACKS	PARTICIPATE IN A RANGER-LED ACTIVITY

The National Park Logo

The National Park System has over 400 units in the US. Just like Badlands National Park, each location is unique or special in some way. The areas include other national parks, historic sites, monuments, seashores, and other recreation areas.

Each element of the National Park emblem represents something that the National Park Service protects. Fill in each blank below to show what each symbol represents.

```
WORD BANK:

MOUNTAINS, ARROWHEAD, BISON,
SEQUOIA TREE, WATER
```

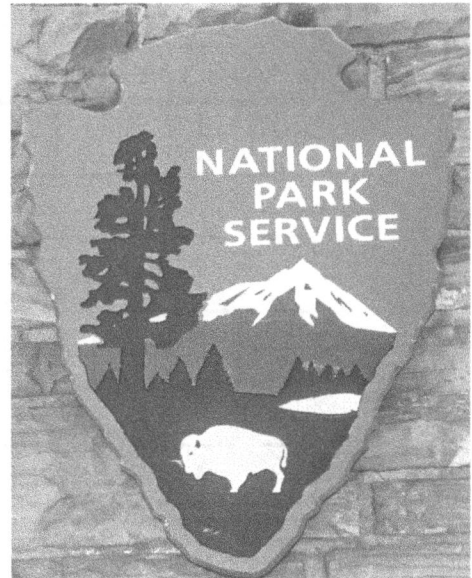

This represents all plants. _____

This represents all animals. _____

This symbol represents the landscapes. _____

This represents the waters protected by the park service. _____

This represents the historical and archeological values. _____

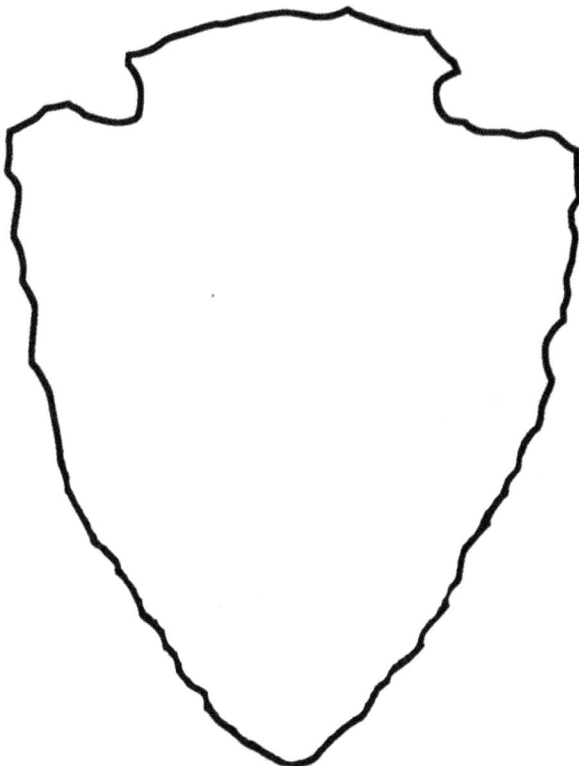

Now it's your turn! Pretend you are designing a new national park. Add elements to the design that represent the things that your park protects

What is the name of your park?

Describe why you included the symbols that you included. What do they mean?

Things to Do Jumble

Unscramble the letters to uncover activities you can do while in Badlands National Park. Hint: each one ends in -ing.

1. SARTGZA ☐☐☐☐☐☐☐☐ ING

2. KHINIG ☐☐☐ ING

3. IRDGNIB ☐☐☐☐ ING

4. NMAGICP ☐☐☐☐ ING

5. KINNICIPCG ☐☐☐☐☐☐☐ ING

6. EINSSTEIGHG ☐☐☐☐☐☐☐☐ ING

7. RABEHOSRCKID ☐☐☐☐☐☐☐☐☐☐☐☐ ING

Word Bank

birding
reading
camping
stargazing
horseback riding
hiking
hunting
singing
yelling
sightseeing
picnicking

Listen to the world around you...

Find a dry piece of ground free of animal poop. Lie on your back and shut your eyes. Make a fist. Every time you hear a sound, put on finger up. When you have 5 fingers up, make a list of all the things you heard.

_____

_____

_____

_____

_____

Review your list. Circle the sounds the belong in the wilderness. Put an X through the ones that don't.

Stop and smell the roses...

Use your nose! Find three things in the park that smell good and three that smell bad. List the things you smelled below.

Good   **Bad**

_____   _____

_____   _____

_____   _____

Review your list. Circle the sounds the belong in the wilderness. Put an X through the ones that don't.

Go Birdwatching at Badlands Wall

start here

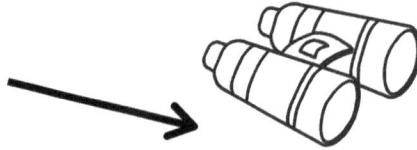

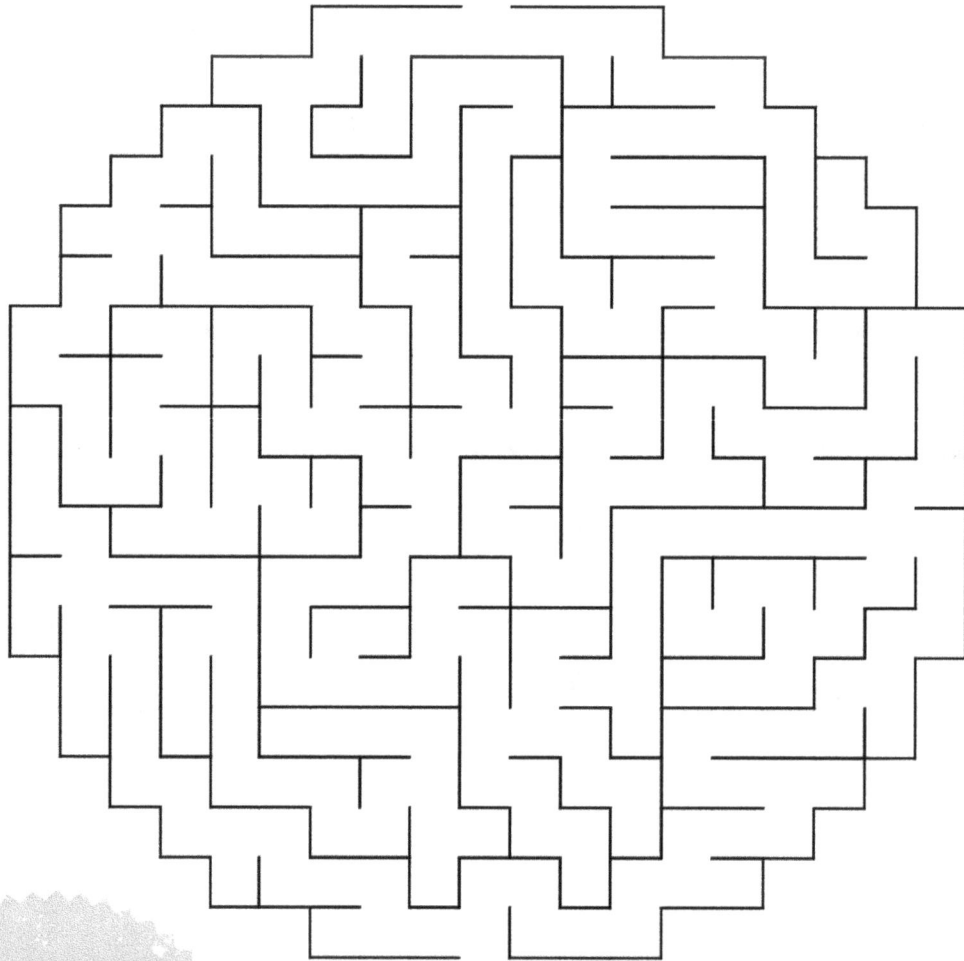

DID YOU KNOW?
Badlands National Park is home to several birds of prey, including golden eagles, short-eared owls and prairie falcons. Birds of prey are birds that hunt other animals for food.

Camping Packing List

What should you take with you camping? Pretend you are in charge of your family camping trip. Make a list of what you would need to be safe and comfortable on an overnight excursion. Some considerations are listed on the side.

1.
2.
3.
4.
5.
6.
7.
8.
9.
10.
11.
12.
13.
14.
15.
16.

- What will you eat at every meal?

- What will the weather be like?

- Where will you sleep?

- What will you do during your free time?

- How luxurious do you want camp to be?

- How will you cook?

- How will you see at night?

- How will you dispose of trash?

- What might you need in case of emergencies?

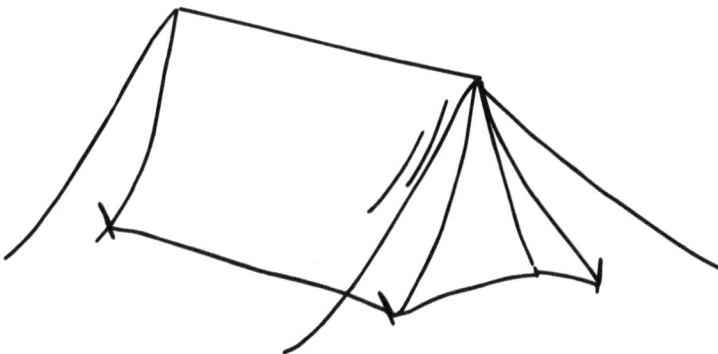

Badlands National Park

Date: _____

Season: _____

Who I went with: _____

Which entrance: _____

How was your experience? Write a few sentences on your trip. Where did you stay? What did you do? What was your favorite activity? If you have not yet visited the park, write a paragraph pretending that you did.

_____

_____

_____

_____

_____

STAMPS

Many national parks and monuments have cancellation stamps for visitors to use. These rubber stamps record the date and the location that you visited. Many people collect the markings as a free souvenir. Check with a ranger to see where you can find a stamp during your visit. If you aren't able to find one, you can draw your own.

Where is the Park?

Badlands National Park is in the great plains region of the United States. It is located in South Dakota, also home to Mount Rushmore!

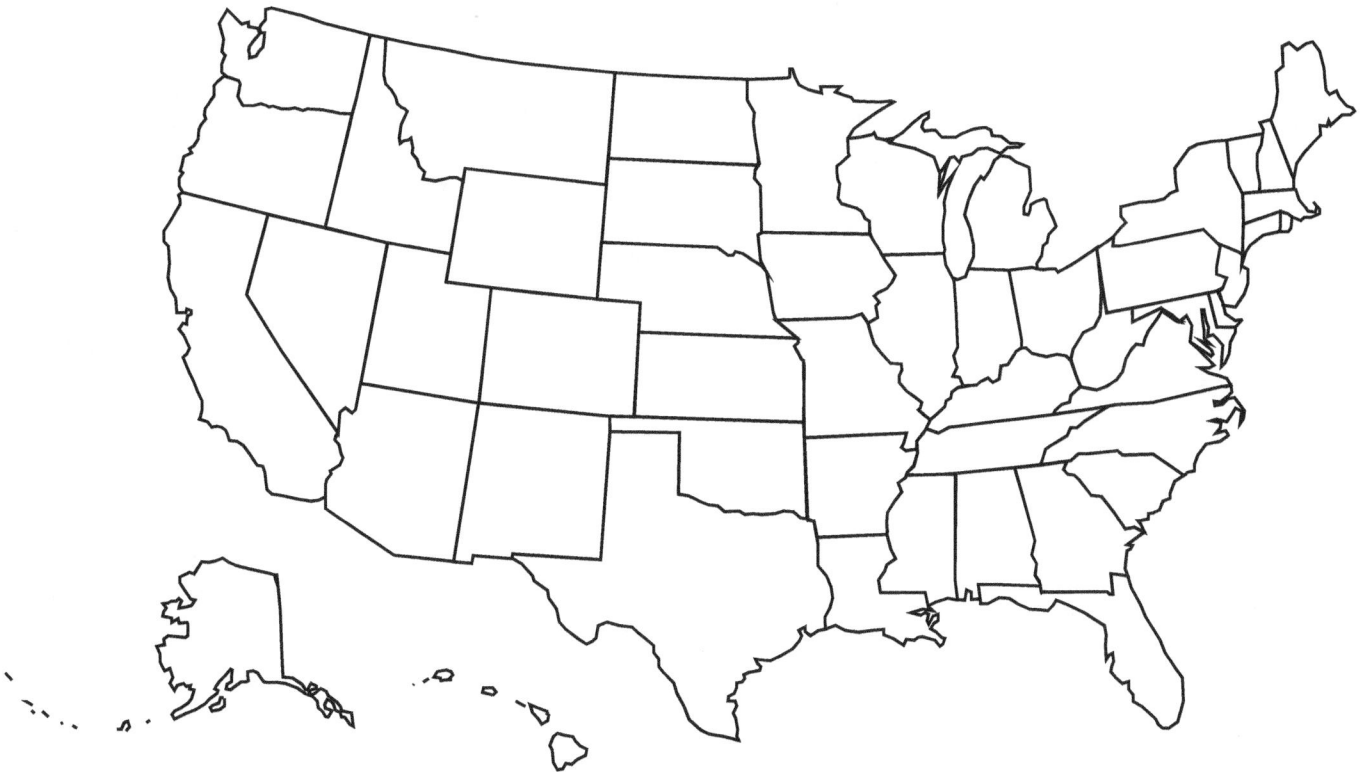

South Dakota

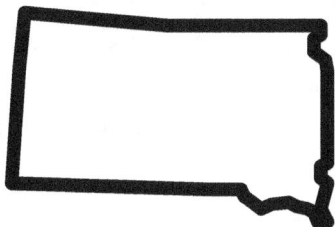

Look at the shape of South Dakota. Can you find it on the map? If you are from the US, can you find your home state? Color South Dakota red. Put a star on the map where you live.

Connect the Dots #1

Connect the dots to figure out what this tiny critter is. There are two types of these that live in Badlands National Park.

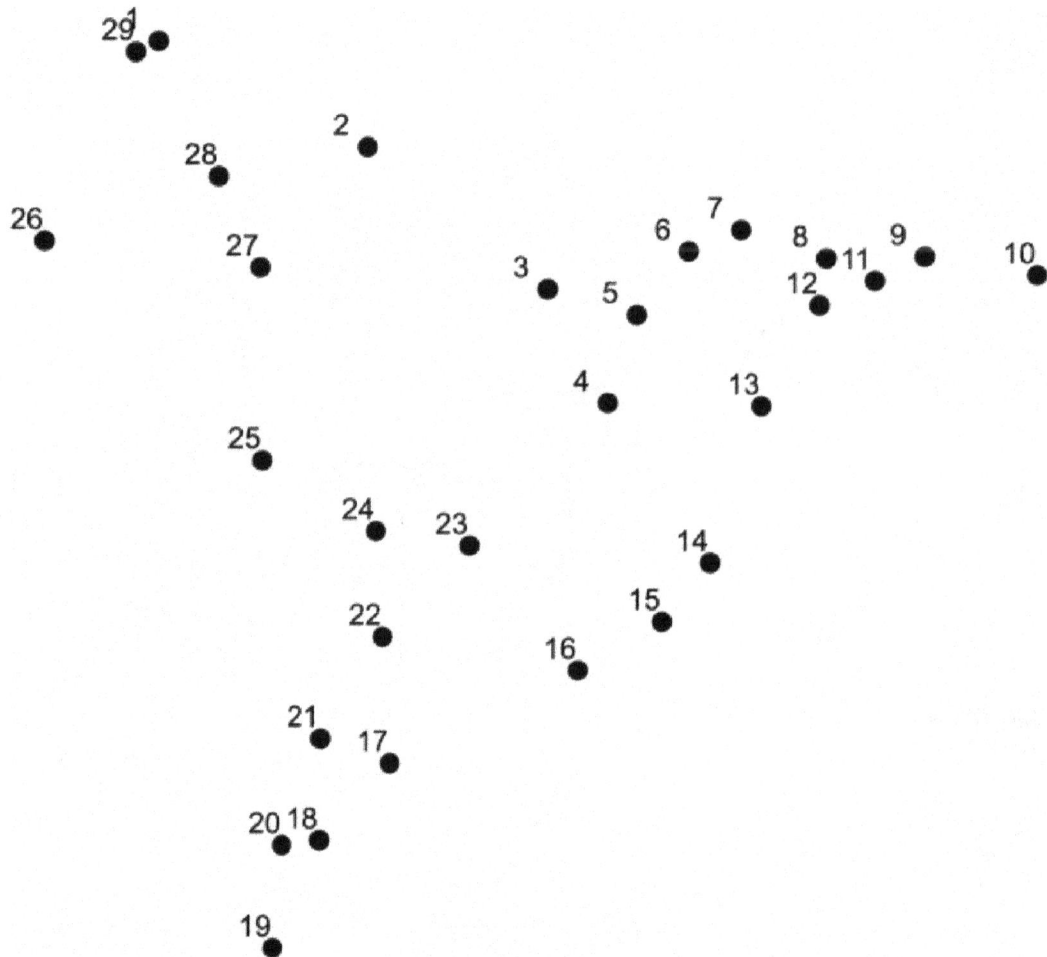

1
29
2
28
26
27
6 7 8 11 9 10
3 12
5
4 13
25
24 23
14
15
22
16
21 17
20 18
19

Their heart rate can reach as high as 1,260 beats per minute and a breathing rate of 250 breaths per minute. Have you ever measured your breathing rate? Ask a friend or family member to set a timer for 60 seconds. Once they say "go", try to breathe normally. Count each breath until they say "stop." How do your breaths per minute compare to hummingbirds?

_____

_____

Garter Snakes are one of the most common snakes in North America. They are generally small to mid-sized and harmless.

American Bison are the largest surviving terrestrial animals in North America. Although commonly referred to as a buffalo in the United States and Canada, it is only distantly related to the true buffalo.

Who lives here?

Here are eight plants and animals that live in the park.
Use the word bank to fill in the clues below.

WORD BANK: BEAVER, CHEATGRASS, KILLDEER, GARTER SNAKE,
BALD EAGLE, BOX ELDER, HORSE, BISON

B ☐ ☐ ☐ ☐

☐ ☐ A ☐ ☐ ☐ ☐ ☐

☐ ☐ D ■ ☐ ☐ ☐ ☐

☐ ☐ L ☐ ☐ ☐

☐ ☐ A ☐ ☐

☐ ☐ ☐ ☐ ☐ ☐ ■ N ☐ ☐

☐ ☐ ☐ ■ ☐ ☐ D ☐ ☐

☐ ☐ ☐ S ☐

While technically the Killdeer is a shorebird, you're more likely to find this bird in an open pasture or parking lot. It is the least water-associated of all shorebirds.

Beavers are the largest North American rodent.

Common Names
vs.
Scientific Names

A common name of an organism is a name that is based on everyday language. You have heard the common names of plants, animals, and other living things on tv, in books, and at school. Common names can also be referred to as "English" names, popular names, or farmer's name. Common names can vary from place to place. The word for a particular tree may be one thing, but that same tree has a different name in another country. Common names can even vary from region to region, even in the same country.

Scientific names, or Latin names, are given to organisms to make it possible to have uniform names for the same species. Scientific names are in Latin. You may have heard plants or animals referred to by their scientific name, or at least parts of their scientific names. Latin names are also called "binomial nomenclature" which refers to a two-part naming system. The first part of the name - the generic name -names the genus to which the species belongs. The second part of the name, the specific name, identifies the species. For example, Tyrannosaurus rex is an example of a widely known scientific name.

American Black Bear

Ursus americanus

COMMON NAME

Elk

Cervus canadensis

LATIN NAME = GENUS + SPECIES

Elk = Cervus canadensis

Black Bear = Ursus americanus

Find the Match!
Common Names and Latin Names

Match the common name to the scientific name for each animal. The first one is done for you. Use clues on the page before and after this one to complete the matches.

Pronghorn   Haliaeetus leucocephalus

Water Plantain   Ovis canadensis

Blue-Eyed Grass   Falco columbarius

Bighorn Sheep   Mustela nigripes

Great Horned Owl   Alisma triviale

Bald Eagle   Crotalus viridis

Merlin   Bubo virginianus

Black-footed Ferret   Antilcapra americana

Prairie Rattlesnake   Sisyrihchium montanum

Bald Eagle
Haliaeetus leucocephalus

Black-footed Ferret
Mustela nigripes

Bald Eagle
Haliaeetus leucocephalus

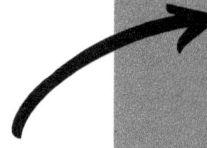

Great Horned Owl
Bubo virginianus

Some plants and animals that live at Badlands

Blue-eyed Grass
Sisyrihchium montanum

Bighorn Sheep
Ovis canadensis

Prairie Rattlesnake
Crotalus viridis

Making a Difference

It is important to protect the valuable resources of the world, not just beautiful places like national parks.

How many of these things do you do at home? If you answered "no" to more than 10 items, talk to the grownups in your life to see if there are any household habits you might be able to change. Conserving our collective resources helps us all.

Yes	No	Do you...
☐	☐	turn off the water when you are brushing your teeth?
☐	☐	use LED light bulbs when possible?
☐	☐	use a reusable water bottle instead of disposable ones?
☐	☐	ride your bike or take the bus instead of riding in the car?
☐	☐	have a rain barrel under your roof gutters to collect rain water?
☐	☐	take quick showers?
☐	☐	avoid putting more food on your plate than you will eat?
☐	☐	take reusable lunch containers?
☐	☐	grow a garden?
☐	☐	buy items with less packaging?
☐	☐	recycle paper?
☐	☐	recycle plastic?
☐	☐	have a compost pile at home so you can make your own soil?
☐	☐	pick up trash when you see it on the trail?
☐	☐	plan a "staycation" and fly only when you have to?

_____   _____
of   # of   Add up your score! Are there any
Yes   No   "no"s that you want to turn into a yes?

Can you think of any other ways to protect our natural resources?

_____

_____ 19

The Ten Essentials

The ten essentials is a list of things that are important to have when you go for longer hikes. If you go on a hike to the **backcountry**, it is especially important that you have everything you need in case of an emergency. If you get lost or something unforeseen happens, it is good to be prepared to survive until help finds you.

The ten essentials list was developed in the 1930s by an outdoors group called the Mountaineers. Over time and technological advancements, this list has evolved. Can you identify all the things on the current list? Circle each of the "essentials" and cross out everything that doesn't make the cut.

fire: matches, lighter, tinder and/or stove	a pint of milk	extra money	headlamp plus extra batteries	extra clothes
extra water	a dog	Polaroid camera	bug net	lightweight games, like a deck of cards
extra food	a roll of duct tape	shelter	sun protection like sunglasses, sun-protective clothes and sunscreen	knife: plus a gear repair kit
a mirror	navigation: map, compass, altimeter, GPS device, or satellite messenger	first aid kit	extra flip-flops	entertainment like video games or books

Backcountry- a remote undeveloped rural area.

Rock Scavenger Hunt

Pay close attention to the things beneath your feet. If you visit Badlands National Park, you will see all sorts of rocks, both big and small. Go on a rock hunt! You may have to get close to the ground and focus carefully to be able to find all the rocks on this list.

- [ ] A sharp rock
- [ ] A flat rock
- [ ] A round rock
- [ ] A rectangular rock
- [ ] A dull rock
- [ ] A rock with stripes
- [ ] A multicolored rock

- [ ] A smooth rock
- [ ] A small rock
- [ ] A huge rock
- [ ] A rough rock
- [ ] A shiny rock
- [ ] A rock with speckles
- [ ] A rock with only one color

Compare two rocks that look very different from each other. What makes them different? Think about their size, their shape, their texture, and their color. Do they have any similarities?

_____

_____

_____

Connect the Dots #2

This animal lives in almost every state in the US, including the national park. They are nocturnal and are more active at night and sleep during the day. They are omnivorous eaters, which means they eat both plants and animals.

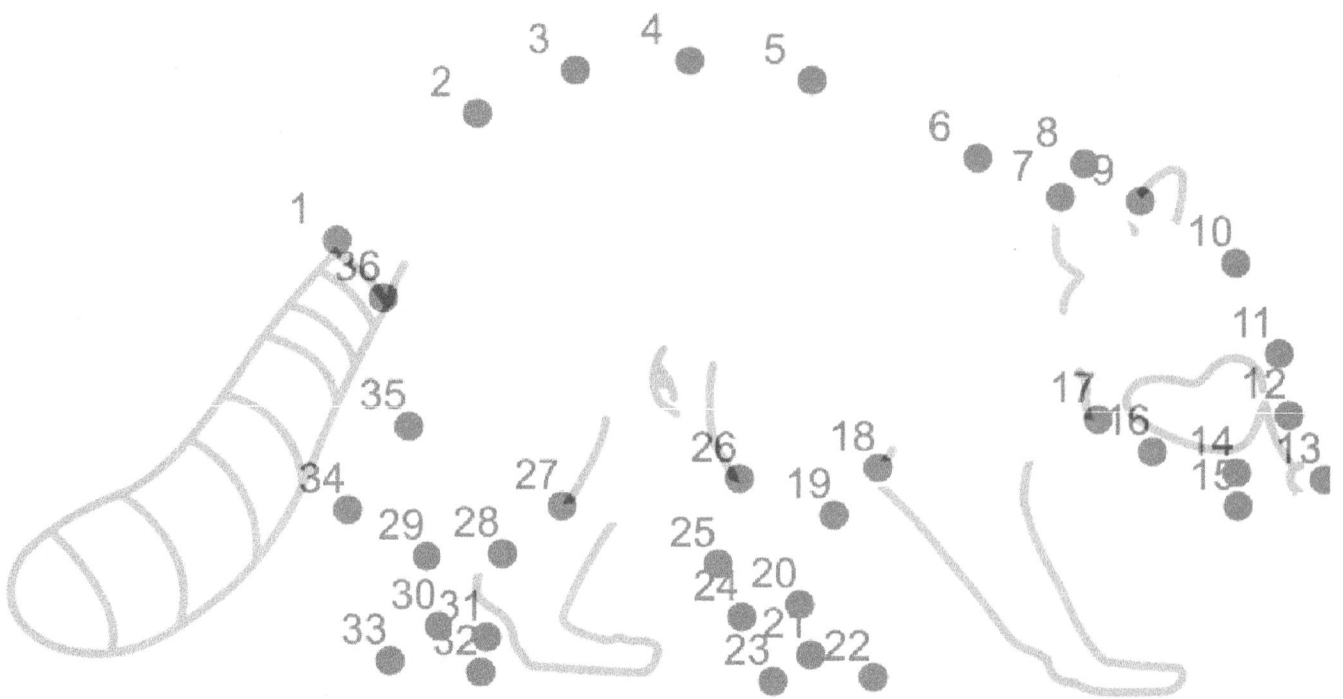

Are you an omnivore like a raccoon? An herbivore only eats plant foods. A carnivore only eats meat. An omnivore eats both. What type of eater are you? Write down some of your favorite foods to back up your answer.

_____

_____

LISTEN CAREFULLY

Visitors to Badlands National Park may hear different noises from those they hear at home. Try this activity to experience this for yourself!

First, find a place outside where it is comfortable to sit or stand for a few minutes. You can do this by yourself or with a friend or family member. Once you have a good spot, close your eyes and listen. Be quiet for one minute and pay attention to what you are hearing. List some of the sounds you have heard in one of the two boxes below:

NATURAL SOUNDS
MADE BY ANIMALS, TREES OR PLANTS, THE WIND, ETC

HUMAN-MADE SOUNDS
MADE BY PEOPLE, MACHINES, ETC

ONCE YOU ARE BACK AT HOME, TRY REPEATING YOUR EXPERIMENT:

NATURAL SOUNDS
MADE BY ANIMALS, TREES OR PLANTS, THE WIND, ETC

HUMAN-MADE SOUNDS
MADE BY PEOPLE, MACHINES, ETC

WHERE DID YOU HEAR MORE NATURAL SOUNDS? _____

WHERE DID YOU HEAR MORE HUMAN SOUNDS? _____

Rain, Rain, Rain

If it rains while you are visiting Badlands National Park, you can do this activity during your trip. If you don't get any rain while you are there, you can follow the same instructions next time it rains where you live.

Go outside into the rain. Use all of your senses as you complete the boxes below. You can use words, drawings, or both.

Sit as still as you can and listen to the rain. How does it make you feel?

Look straight up at the sky and let the raindrops fall on your face. Close your eyes. How does it feel?

Watch where the rain goes. Pay attention to the different surfaces the rain lands on. Which surfaces absorb the rain, and which surfaces cause the rain to run off or pool?

Are there any animals or bugs out enjoying the rain? Do you think the plants are enjoying the rain?

Badlands Word Search

Words may be horizontal, vertical, or diagonal
and they might be backward!

1. badland
2. bison
3. erosion
4. south dakota
5. prairie dog
6. fossil
7. lakota
8. sunset
9. pronghorn
10. grasslands
11. sage creek
12. hiking
13. ferret
14. rattlesnake
15. stargazing
16. sunrise
17. butte
18. bighorn

```
S  W  B  I  G  H  O  R  N  S  K  L  F  W  K
N  O  S  I  B  I  L  E  S  H  E  O  W  R  J
T  E  U  R  K  A  O  R  C  C  S  B  A  P  B
S  M  P  T  E  R  R  E  F  S  R  L  U  U  R
C  E  A  I  H  H  I  K  I  N  G  U  T  K  A
A  O  L  D  Y  D  S  L  D  B  T  T  A  C  T
R  O  A  D  P  R  A  I  R  I  E  D  O  G  T
P  S  B  S  S  E  G  K  G  W  E  I  R  X  L
R  T  H  S  U  E  E  R  O  S  I  O  N  P  E
E  A  I  C  N  N  C  Y  H  T  N  G  O  R  S
Q  R  A  H  S  C  R  C  N  N  A  E  N  O  N
S  G  N  I  E  M  E  I  S  M  O  K  I  N  A
L  A  K  O  T  A  E  S  S  J  R  A  Q  G  K
J  Z  G  T  L  E  K  E  S  E  O  R  V  H  E
N  I  X  A  K  B  A  D  L  A  N  D  H  O  M
X  N  T  F  A  R  E  G  L  Z  E  S  Q  R  E
U  G  R  A  S  S  L  A  N  D  S  P  V  N  B
C  J  D  O  S  R  E  D  N  Y  M  A  L  A  S
```

25

Find the Match!
What are Baby Animals Called?

Match the animal to its baby. The first one is done for you.

Elk	eaglet
Bald Eagle	calf
Little Brown Bat	snakelets
Striped Skunk	pup
Great Horned Owl	owlet
Western Toad	kit
Mountain Lion	tadpole
Garter snake	kitten

Color the Badlands

Badlands are a type of terrain where softer clay-rich soils and sedimentary rocks have eroded. Badlands are found on every continent except Antarctica. Badlands National Park has extensive formations of badlands.

The Perfect Picnic Spot

Fill in the blanks on this page without looking at the full story. Once you have each line filled out, use the words you've chosen to complete the story on the next page.

EMOTION _____

FOOD _____

SOMETHING SWEET _____

STORE _____

MODE OF TRANSPORTATION _____

NOUN _____

SOMETHING ALIVE _____

SAUCE _____

PLURAL VEGETABLES _____

ADJECTIVE _____

PLURAL BODY PART _____

ANIMAL _____

PLURAL FRUIT _____

PLACE _____

SOMETHING TALL _____

COLOR _____

ADJECTIVE _____

NOUN _____

A DIFFERENT ANIMAL _____

FAMILY MEMBER #1 _____

FAMILY MEMBER #2 _____

VERB THAT ENDS IN -ING _____

A DIFFERENT FOOD _____

The Perfect Picnic Spot

Use the words from the previous page to complete a silly story.

When my family suggested having our lunch at the Conata Picnic Area, I was

_ _ _ _ _ _ _ _. I love eating my _ _ _ _ _ _ outside! I knew we had picked up a
EMOTION   FOOD

box of _ _ _ _ _ _ from the _ _ _ _ _ _ _ _ for after lunch, my favorite. We drove up to
SOMETHING SWEET   STORE

the area and I jumped out of the _ _ _ _ _ _ _ _. "I will find the perfect spot for a
                   MODE OF TRANSPORTATION

picnic!" I grabbed a _ _ _ _ _ _ for us to sit on, and I ran off. I passed a picnic table,
            NOUN

but it was covered with _ _ _ _ _ _ _ _ so we couldn't sit there. The next picnic table
            SOMETHING ALIVE

looked okay, but there were smears of _ _ _ _ _ _ and pieces of _ _ _ _ _ _ _ _
                   SAUCE   PLURAL VEGETABLES

everywhere. The people that were there before must have been _ _ _ _ _ _! I gritted
                              ADJECTIVE

my _ _ _ _ _ _ _ together and kept walking down the path, determined to find the
PLURAL BODY PART

perfect spot. I wanted a table with a good view of the geologic formations. Why

was this so hard? If we were lucky, I might even get to see _ _ _ _ _ _ eating some
                           ANIMAL

_ _ _ _ _ _ on the cliffside. They don't have those in _ _ _ _ _ _ _ where I am from. I
PLURAL FRUIT   PLACE

walked down a little hill and there it was, the perfect spot! The trees towered

overhead and looked as tall as _ _ _ _ _ _ _ _. The patch of grass was a beautiful
                   SOMETHING TALL

_ _ _ _ _ _ color. The _ _ _ _ _ _ flowers were growing on
COLOR   ADJECTIVE

the side of a _ _ _ _ _ _. I looked across the geologic formations edge and even saw
          NOUN

a _ _ _ _ _ _ _ _ on the edge of a rock. I looked back to see my _ _ _ _ _ _ _ _ and
DIFFERENT ANIMAL   FAMILY MEMBER #1

_ _ _ _ _ _ _ _ _ _ _ _ _ _ a picnic basket. "I hope you brought plenty of
FAMILY MEMBER #2   VERB THAT ENDS IN ING

_ _ _ _ _ _ _, I'm starving!"
A DIFFERENT FOOD

Hike the Fossil Exhibit Trail!

start here →

DID YOU KNOW?
Over 13,000 bones and over 300 archaeological sites have have been excavated within the park. If you find a fossil, be sure to let a park ranger know!

The Geologic Formations of the Badlands

The formations in Badlands National Park and badlands formations around the world are the end-product of two simple processes: **deposition** and **erosion**. Deposition is the process of rocks gradually building up. Erosion is the process of rocks gradually wearing away. These rocks have much to teach us about Earth's history.

1. sandstone
2. siltstone
3. volcanic ash
4. butte
5. shale
6. canyon
7. ridge
8. Yellow Mounds
9. Chandron
10. Brule
11. Sharps
12. Rockyford Ash
13. erosion
14. deposition
15. eruption
16. fossils
17. Big Pig Dig
18. river

```
L E R O S I O N H B D N O W S
H A D A A I A Z S I E O W R H
T V D N N I T T A G A I K O A
C H A N D R O N C P U T B C R
C F N A S H A L E I Y I S K P
M O D V T R R K C G A S I Y S
C S S E O R C E R D O O L F N
A S B E N L I R D I L P V O B
L I H O E I C O E G U E E R N
L L I R S M O A K E U D U D O
I S I L T S T O N E K L N A I
S C N S K A O I S I E K T S T
T A O S F H I N Z I C L W H P
E N R E L I V E I B D A V E U
R Y E L L O W M O U N D S E R
T O V L G R E E N T A K E H E
U N I E S A E N N T A P V E B
C J R I D G E E R E Y S I O N
```

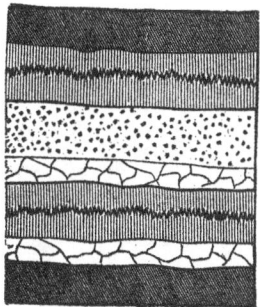

31

Leave No Trace Quiz

Leave No Trace is a concept that helps people make decisions during outdoor recreation that protects the environment. There are seven principles that guide us when we spend time outdoors, whether you are in a national park or not. Are you an expert in Leave No Trace? Take this quiz and find out!

1. How can you plan ahead and prepare to ensure you have the best experience you can in the national park?
   a. Make sure you stop by the ranger station for a map and to ask about current conditions.
   b. Just wing it! You will know the best trail when you see it.
   c. Stick to your plan, even if conditions change. You traveled a long way to get here, and you should stick to your plan.

2. What is an example of traveling on a durable surface?
   a. Walking only on the designated path.
   b. Walking on the grass that borders the trail if the trail is very muddy.
   c. Taking a shortcut if you can find one since it means you will be walking less.

3. Why should you dispose of waste properly?
   a. You don't need to. Park rangers love to pick up the trash you leave behind.
   b. You actually should leave your leftovers behind, because animals will eat them. It is important to make sure they aren't hungry.
   c. So that other peoples' experiences of the park are not impacted by you leaving your waste behind.

4. How can you best follow the concept "leave what you find"?
   a. Take only a small rock or leaf to remember your trip.
   b. Take pictures, but leave any physical items where they are.
   c. Leave everything you find, unless it may be rare like an arrowhead, then it is okay to take.

5. What is not a good example of minimizing campfire impacts?
   a. Only having a campfire in a pre-existing campfire ring.
   b. Checking in with current conditions when you consider making a campfire.
   c. Building a new campfire ring in a location that has a better view.

6. What is a poor example of respecting wildlife?
   a. Building squirrel houses out of rocks so the squirrels have a place to live.
   b. Stay far away from wildlife and give them plenty of space.
   c. Reminding your grown-ups to not drive too fast in animal habitats while visiting the park.

7. How can you show consideration of other visitors?
   a. Play music on your speaker so other people at the campground can enjoy it.
   b. Wear headphones on the trail if you choose to listen to music.
   c. Make sure to yell "Hello!" to every animal you see at top volume.

Park Poetry

America's parks inspire art of all kinds. Painters, sculptors, photographers, writers, and artists of all mediums have taken inspiration from natural beauty. They have turned their inspiration into great works.

Use this space to write your own poem about the park. Think about what you have experienced or seen. Use descriptive language to create an acrostic poem. This type of poem has the first letter of each line spell out another word. Create an acrostic that spells out the word "Bison."

B _____

I _____

S _____

O _____

N _____

Birds

Interesting fossils

So much grass

On the butte

Nothing but rocks

Big rocks

In the dirt

Stories told

Open skies

Nature all around

Reflections on Special Places

National parks are special places for all sorts of reasons. Can you think of an outdoor area that is special to you? It can be a place you love because your family is from there, or because it is beautiful, or because you can do your favorite things there.

What is a place (does not have to be a national park) that is special to you?

_____

_____

_____

_____

What do national parks mean to you?

_____

_____

_____

What is your favorite part of being able to enjoy the national parks around you?

_____

_____

_____

Spot the Wildlife at Robert's Prairie Dog Town!

start here

PRO-TIP

Seeing animals in the wild can be so exciting! It is important to remember to keep a minimum of 100 yards between you any wildlife you see!

Stacking Rocks

Have you ever seen stacks of rocks while hiking in national parks? Do you know what they are or what they mean? These rock piles are called cairns and often mark hiking routes in parks. Every park has a different way to maintain trails and cairns. However, they all have the same rule: If you come across a cairn, do not disturb it.

Color the cairn and the rules to remember.

1. Do not tamper with cairns.

If a cairn is tampered with or an unauthorized one is built, then future visitors may become disoriented or even lost.

2. Do not build unauthorized cairns.

Moving rocks disturbs the soil and makes the area more prone to erosion. Disturbing rocks can disturb fragile plants.

3. Do not add to existing cairns.

Authorized cairns are carefully designed. Adding to them can actually cause them to collapse.

Decoding Using American Sign Language

American Sign Language, also called ASL for short, is a language that many Deaf people or people who are hard of hearing use to communicate. People use ASL to communicate with their hands. Did you know people from all over the country and world travel to national parks? You may hear people speaking other languages. You might also see people using ASL. Use the American Manual Alphabet chart to decode some national parks facts.

This was the first national park to be established:

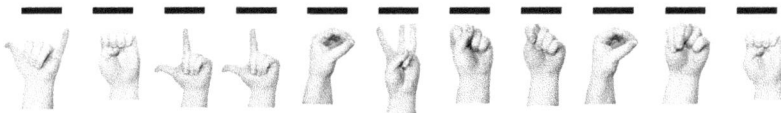

_ _ _ _ _ _ _ _ _ _

This is the biggest national park in the US:

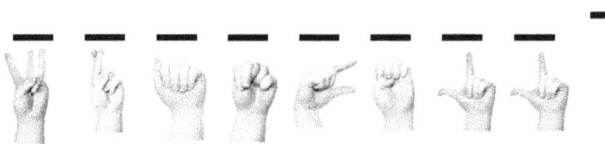

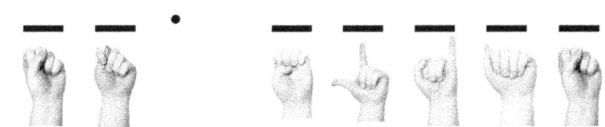

_ _ _ _ _ _ _ -

_ _ . _ _ _ _

This is the most visited national park:

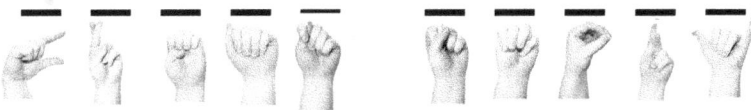

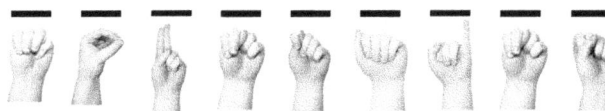

_ _ _ _ _ _ _ _

_ _ _ _ _ _ _ _

Aa	Bb	Cc	Dd	Ee
Ff	Gg		Hh	Ii
Jj	Kk	Ll	Mm	Nn
Oo	Pp		Qq	Rr
Ss	Tt		Uu	Vv
Ww	Xx		Yy	Zz

Hint: Pay close attention to the position of the thumb!

Try it! Using the chart, try to make the letters of the alphabet with your hand. What is the hardest letter to make? Can you spell out your name? Show a friend or family member and have them watch you spell out the name of the national park you are in.

Go Horseback Riding at the Sage Creek Campground

Help find the horse's lost shoe!

start here

DID YOU KNOW?

There are no marked trails for horseback riding, allowing for horse owners to explore all 64,000 acres of the Badlands Wilderness Area!

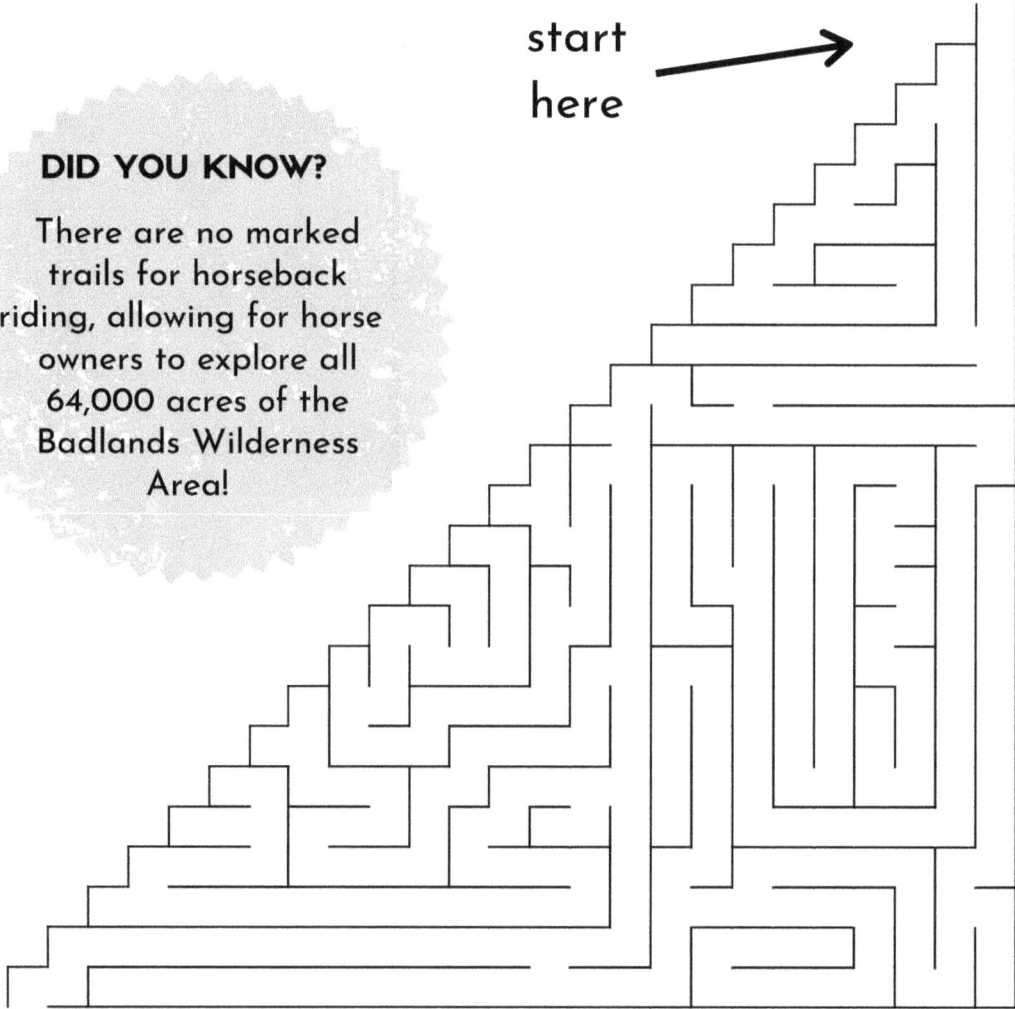

Butterflies of the Badlands

Sixty-nine species of butterflies and moths live in Badlands National Park. Their wingspan size varies, as do the patterns on their wings. Design your own butterfly below. Make sure the wings are symmetrical, meaning both sides match.

A Hike at Notch Trail

Fill in the blanks on this page without looking at the full story. Once you have each line filled out, use the words you've chosen to complete the story on the next page.

ADJECTIVE _____

SOMETHING TO EAT _____

SOMETHING TO DRINK _____

NOUN _____

ARTICLE OF CLOTHING _____

BODY PART _____

VERB _____

ANIMAL _____

SAME TYPE OF FOOD _____

ADJECTIVE _____

SAME ANIMAL _____

VERB THAT ENDS IN "ED" _____

NUMBER _____

A DIFFERENT NUMBER _____

SOMETHING THAT FLIES _____

LIGHT SOURCE _____

PLURAL NOUN _____

FAMILY MEMBER _____

YOUR NICKNAME _____

A Hike at Notch Trail

Use the words from the previous page to complete a silly story.

I went for a hike at Notch Trail today. In my favorite _ _ _ _ _ _ _ backpack, I
                                                        ADJECTIVE

made sure to pack a map so I wouldn't get lost. I also threw in an extra

_ _ _ _ _ _ _ _ _ _ _ just in case I got hungry and a bottle of _ _ _ _ _ _ _ _ _ _. I put
SOMETHING TO EAT   SOMETHING TO DRINK

on my _ _ _ _ _ _ _ _ _ spray, and a tied a _ _ _ _ _ _ _ _ _ _ _ _ around my
       NOUN   ARTICLE OF CLOTHING

_ _ _ _ _ _ _ _ _ _, in case it gets chilly. I started to _ _ _ _ _ _ down the path. As
BODY PART   VERB

soon as I turned the corner, I came face to face with a(n) _ _ _ _ _ _ _ _. I think
                                                          ANIMAL

it was as startled as I was! What should I do? I had to think fast! Should I

give it some of my _ _ _ _ _ _ _ _ _ _ _? No. I had to remember what the
                   SAME TYPE OF FOOD

_ _ _ _ _ _ _ ranger told me. "If you see one, back away slowly and try not to
ADJECTIVE

scare it." Soon enough, the _ _ _ _ _ _ _ _ _ _   _ _ _ _ _ _ _ _ _ _ away. The coast
                           SAME ANIMAL   VERB THAT ENDS IN ED

was clear. _ _ _ _ _ _ hours later, I finally got to the lookout. I felt like I could
           NUMBER

see for a _ _ _ _ _ _ miles. I took a picture of a _ _ _ _ _ _ _ _ so I could always
          A DIFFERENT NUMBER   NOUN

remember this moment. As I was putting my camera away, a _ _ _ _ _ _ _ _ _
                                                         SOMETHING THAT FLIES

flew by, reminding me that it was almost nighttime. I turned on my

_ _ _ _ _ _ _ _ _ _ and headed back. I could hear the _ _ _ _ _ _ _ _ _ _ singing their
LIGHT SOURCE   PLURAL INSECT

evening song. Just as I was getting tired, I saw my _ _ _ _ _ _ _ _ _ and our tent.
                                                    FAMILY MEMBER

"Welcome back _ _ _ _ _ _ _! How was your hike?"
              NICKNAME

Snail Mail

Design a postcard to send to a friend or a family member. Who do you want to tell about Badlands National Park? In the first template, write your message. In the second template, create a design for the front of the postcard. You could show something you saw, something you did, or something you want to do in the national park.

Postcard

Let's Go Camping
Word Search

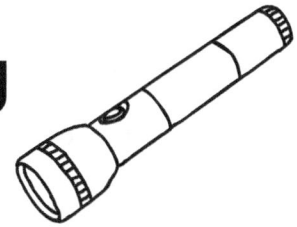

Words may be horizontal, vertical, or diagonal and they might be backward!

1. tent
2. camp stove
3. sleeping bag
4. bug spray
5. sunscreen
6. map
7. flashlight
8. pillow
9. lantern
10. ice
11. snacks
12. smores
13. water
14. first aid kit
15. chair
16. cards
17. books
18. games
19. trail
20. hat

```
D P P I L L O W D B T E A C I
E O A D P R E A A M B R C A N
P W C A M P S T O V E I H X G
R A H S G E L E B E E D A P S
E L B U G S P R A Y N G I E A
S I A H G C I C N N M E R C N
C W N L A F I R S K O O B F K
M T A E M I L E L H M R W L J
T A P R E A O R E S L B A A B
S M P A S R R T E N T L U S C
C E A I I R C G P E I U J H A
S S N A C K S S I M O K I L R
I J R S F O I S N J R A Q I D
C Y E T L E V E G U O R V G S
E W T A K C A B B S S O H H M
X J N F I R S T A I D K I T T
U A A E S S E N G E T P V A B
C J L I A R T D N A M A H A S
```

43

All in the Day of a Park Ranger

Park Rangers are hardworking individuals dedicated to protecting our parks, monuments, museums, and more. They take care of the natural and cultural resources for future generations. Rangers also help protect the visitors of the park. Their responsibilities are broad and they work both with the public and behind the scenes.

What have you seen park rangers do? Use your knowledge of the duties of park rangers to fill out a typical daily schedule, one activity for each hour. Feel free to make up your own, but some examples of activities are provided on the right. Read carefully, not all of the example activities are befitting a ranger!

Time	Activity	Examples
6 am	Lead a sunrise hike	• feed the bald eagles
7 am		• build trails for visitors to enjoy
8 am		• throw rocks off the side of the mountain
9 am		• rescue lost hikers
10 am		• study animal behavior
11 am		• record air quality data
12 pm	Enjoy a lunch break outside	• answer questions at the visitor center
1 pm		• pick wildflowers
2 pm		• pick up litter
3 pm		• share marshmallows with squirrels
4 pm	Teach visitors about the geology of the mountain	• repair handrails
5 pm		• lead a class on a field trip
6 pm		• catch frogs and make them race
7 pm		• lead people on educational hikes
8 pm		• write articles for the park website
9 pm		• protect the river from pollution

Additional examples:
• remove non-native plants from the park
• study how climate change is affecting the park
• give a talk about mountain lions
• lead a program for campers on salmon

If you were a park ranger, which of the above tasks would you enjoy most?

_____

_____

Draw Yourself as a Park Ranger

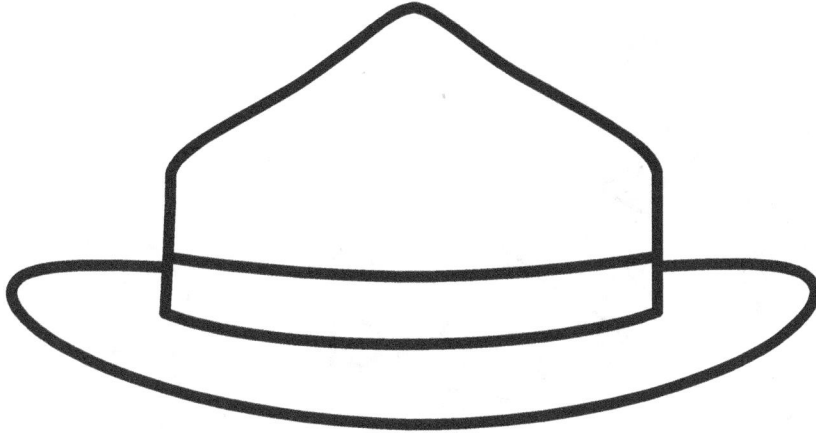

RANGER

The Fish of the Badlands

Unscramble these common fish names that live in the park.

1.
YEGLDOE

2.
PACR

3.
WNOINM

4.
LHEDALUB

5.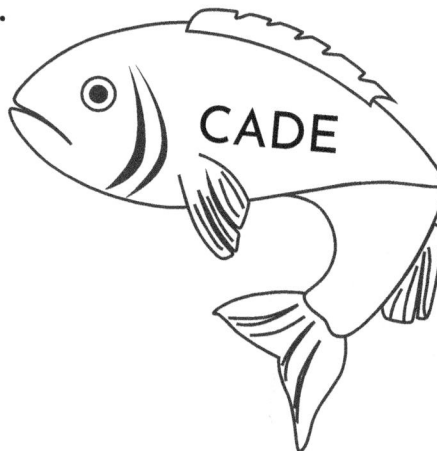
CADE

1. _____
2. _____
3. _____
4. _____
5. _____

Word Bank

carp
shiner
goldeye
minnow
bullhead
sauger
redhorse
dace

Amphibians

Three species of toads and one species of frog live in Badlands Park. There's even one type of Salamander there, too. Frogs and toads both spend the beginning of their lives the same way, as tadpoles. Tadpoles hatch from eggs in water, usually in springs or pools of water.

Both frogs and toads are amphibians. Salamanders are amphibians too. Color the amphibians below.

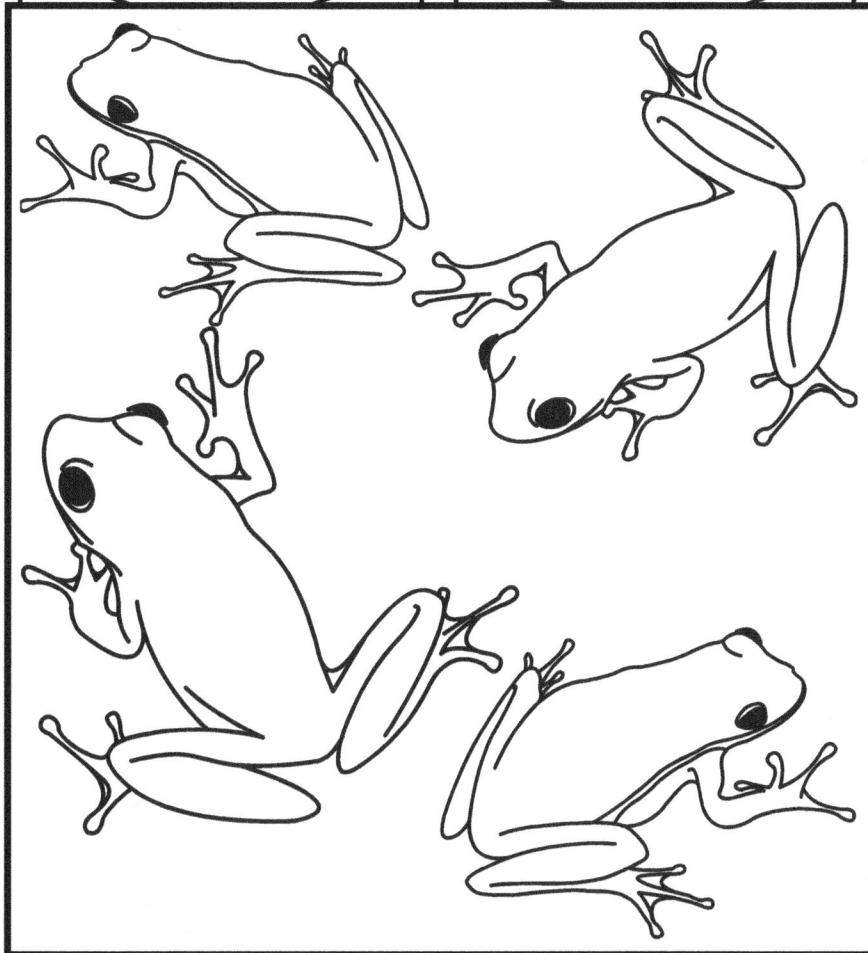

Weather Watch

Find a place where you are in an open area where you can easily see the sky. Complete the activities below to provide your weather report. If you aren't in the park, you can do this activity from home.

Can you feel any wind?

What does the sky look like?

Is there anything you notice about the weather today?

What is the date?

What is the time?

Where is the sun in the sky? (rising, midpoint, falling)

What direction is the wind blowing?

Are there clouds in the sky? If so, draw them below:

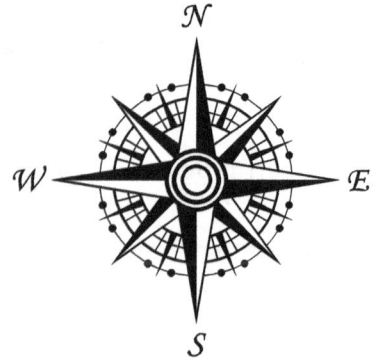

Help Protect Endangered Species

Badlands National Park is home to the endangered Black-footed Ferret. Create a magazine article that would encourage people to help protect an endangered species.

63 National Parks

How many other national parks have you been to? Which one do you want to visit next? Note that some of these parks fall on the border of more than one state, you may check it off more than once!

Alaska
☐ Denali National Park
☐ Gates of the Arctic National Park
☐ Glacier Bay National Park
☐ Katmai National Park
☐ Kenai Fjords National Park
☐ Kobuk Valley National Park
☐ Lake Clark National Park
☐ Wrangell-St. Elias National Park

American Samoa
☐ National Park of American Samoa

Arizona
☐ Grand Canyon National Park
☐ Petrified Forest National Park
☐ Saguaro National Park

Arkansas
☐ Hot Springs National Park

California
☐ Channel Islands National Park
☐ Death Valley National Park
☐ Joshua Tree National Park
☐ Kings Canyon National Park
☐ Lassen Volcanic National Park
☐ Pinnacles National Park
☐ Redwood National Park
☐ Sequoia National Park
☐ Yosemite National Park

Colorado
☐ Black Canyon of the Gunnison National Park
☐ Great Sand Dunes National Park
☐ Mesa Verde National Park
☐ Rocky Mountain National Park

Florida
☐ Biscayne National Park
☐ Dry Tortugas National Park
☐ Everglades National Park

Hawaii
☐ Haleakala National Park
☐ Hawai'i Volcanoes National Park

Idaho
☐ Yellowstone National Park

Kentucky
☐ Mammoth Cave National Park

Indiana
☐ Indiana Dunes National Park

Maine
☐ Acadia National Park

Michigan
☐ Isle Royale National Park

Minnesota
☐ Voyageurs National Park

Missouri
☐ Gateway Arch National Park

Montana
☐ Glacier National Park
☐ Yellowstone National Park

Nevada
☐ Death Valley National Park
☐ Great Basin National Park

New Mexico
☐ Carlsbad Caverns National Park
☐ White Sands National Park

North Dakota
☐ Theodore Roosevelt National Park

North Carolina
☐ Great Smoky Mountains National Park

Ohio
☐ Cuyahoga Valley National Park

Oregon
☐ Crater Lake National Park

South Carolina
☐ Congaree National Park

South Dakota
☐ Badlands National Park
☐ Wind Cave National Park

Tennessee
☐ Great Smoky Mountains National Park

Texas
☐ Big Bend National Park
☐ Guadalupe Mountains National Park

Utah
☐ Arches National Park
☐ Bryce Canyon National Park
☐ Canyonlands National Park
☐ Capitol Reef National Park
☐ Zion National Park

Virgin Islands
☐ Virgin Islands National Park

Virginia
☐ Shenandoah National Park

Washington
☐ Mount Rainier National Park
☐ North Cascades National Park
☐ Olympic National Park

West Virginia
☐ New River Gorge National Park

Wyoming
☐ Grand Teton National Park
☐ Yellowstone National Park

Other National Parks

Besides Badlands National Park, there are 62 other diverse and beautiful national parks across the United States. Try your hand at this crossword. If you need help, look at the previous page for some hints.

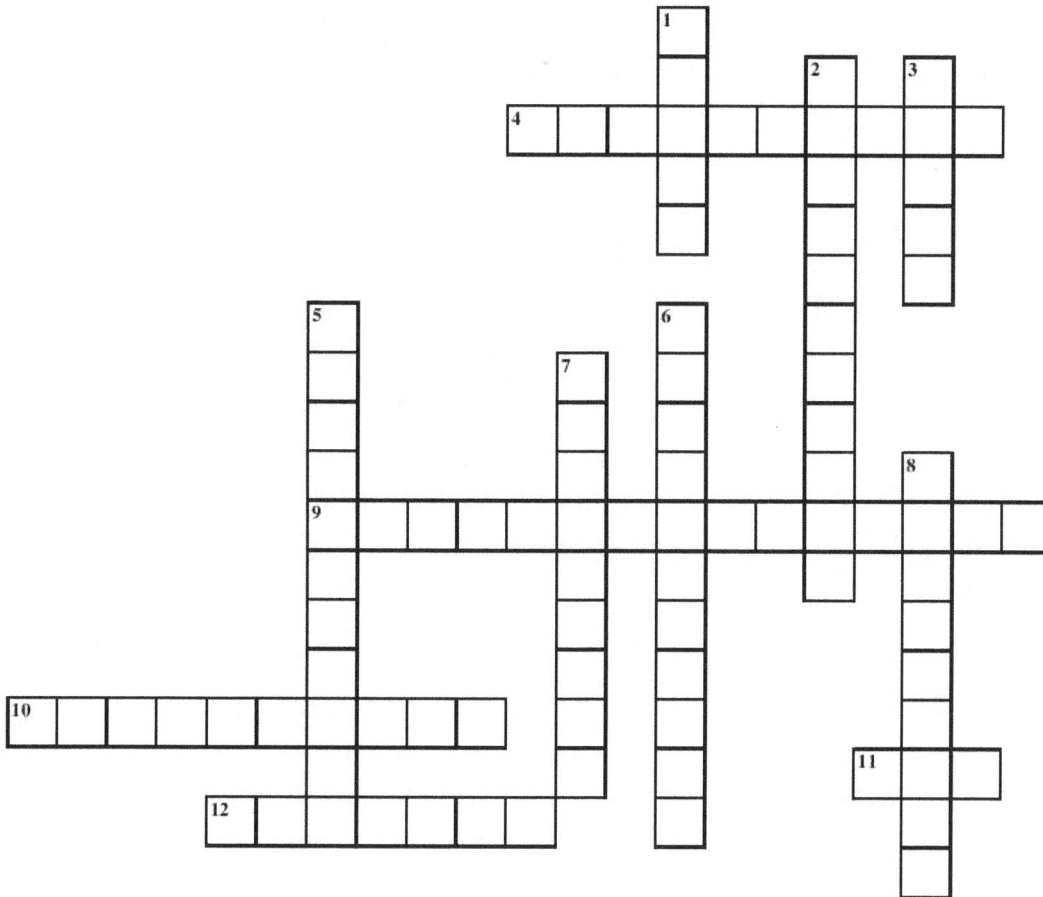

Down

1. State where Acadia National Park is located
2. This national park has the Spanish word for turtle in it.
3. Number of national parks in Alaska
5. This national park has some of the hottest temperatures in the world.
6. This national park is the only one in Idaho.
7. This toothsome creature can be famously found in Everglades National Park.
8. Only president with a national park named for them

Across

4. This state has the most national parks.
9. This park has some of the newest land in the US, caused by volcanic eruptions.
10. This park has the deepest lake in the United States.
11. This color shows up in the name of a national park in California.
12. This national park deserves a gold medal.

Which National Park Will You Go to Next? Word Search

1. Zion
2. Big Bend
3. Glacier
4. Olympic
5. Sequoia
6. Bryce
7. Mesa Verde
8. Biscayne
9. Wind Cave
10. Great Basin
11. Katmai
12. Yellowstone
13. Voyageurs
14. Arches
15. Badlands
16. Denali
17. Glacier Bay
18. Hot Springs

```
F M M E S A V E R D E B N E Y
E A B I G B E N D E S A S E M
Y L I C A L O Y N E E D L T G
D M G A S S A U C N R L U E R
C E L I I T S C R E O A A K E
S N A W Y E E O I W T N A C A
G I C H A A Q C S E M D N S T
N O I Z P R U T I M R S N E B
I W E L M P O N B W E B K H A
R J R F D N I F L I H B U C S
P A B E E S A N E S O P W R I
S J A E N Y A C S I B A U A N
T C Y I A D O H H Y M E A L R
O T A T L M L E S E G R W R J
H S T O I K A T M A I R O P B
I C H U R C O L Y M P I C O U
O Y G T S D E O S B R Y C E T
W I N D C A V E I N R O H E M
```

52

Field Notes

Spend some time to reflect on your trip to Badlands National Park. Your field notes will help you remember the things you experienced. Use the space below to write about your day.

While I was at Badlands National Park...

I saw:

_____

_____

_____

_____

I heard:

_____

_____

_____

_____

I felt:

_____

_____

_____

_____

I wondered:

_____

_____

_____

_____

Draw a picture of your favorite thing in the park.

ANSWER KEY

National Park Emblem Answers

1. This represents all plants. **Sequoia Tree**

2. This represents all animals. **Bison**

3. This symbol represents the landscapes. **Mountains**

4. This represents the waters protected by the park service. **Water**

5. This represents the historical and archeological values. **Arrowhead**

Jumbles Answers

1. STARGAZING

2. HIKING

3. BIRDING

4. CAMPING

5. PICNICKING

6. SIGHTSEEING

7. HORSEBACK RIDING

Go Birdwatching at Badlands Wall

start
here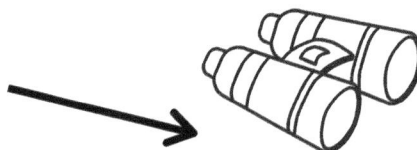

DID YOU KNOW?
Badlands National Park
is home to several birds
of prey, including
golden eagles, short-
eared owls and prairie
falcons. Birds of prey
are birds that hunt
other animals for food.

Answers: Who lives here?

Here are eight plants and animals that live in the park.
Use the word bank to fill in the clues below.

WORD BANK: BEAVER, CHEATGRASS, KILLDEER, GARTER SNAKE,
BALD EAGLE, BOX ELDER, HORSE, BISON

B ISON

CHE A TGRASS

BAL D ■EAGLE

KIL L DEER

BE A VER

GARTER ■ SN AKE

BOX ■ EL D ER

HOR S E

Find the Match!
Common Names and Latin Names

Match the common name to the scientific name for each animal. The first one is done for you. Use clues on the page before and after this one to complete the matches.

Ponghorn   Haliaeetus leucocephalus

Water Plantain   Ovis canadensis

Blue-eyed Grass   Falco columbarius

Bighorn Sheep   Mustela nigripes

Great Horned Owl   Alisma triviale

Bald Eagle   Crotalus viridi

Merlin   Bubo virginianus

Black-footed Ferret   Antilcapra americana

Prairie Rattlesnake   Sisyrihchium montanum

Bald Eagle

Haliaeetus leucocephalus

Answers: The Ten Essentials

The ten essentials is a list of things that are important to have when you go for longer hikes. If you go on a hike to the <u>backcountry</u>, it is especially important that you have everything you need in case of an emergency. If you get lost or something unforeseen happens, it is good to be prepared to survive until help finds you.

The ten essentials list was developed in the 1930s by an outdoors group called the Mountaineers. Over time and technological advancements, this list has evolved. Can you identify all the things on the current list? Circle each of the "essentials" and cross out everything that doesn't make the cut.

(fire: matches, lighter, tinder and/or stove)	a pair of milk	extra money	(headlamp plus extra batteries)	(extra clothes)
(extra water)	a dog	Polaroid camera	bug net	lightweight games like a deck of cards
(extra food)	a roll of duct tape	(shelter)	(sun protection like sunglasses, sun-protective clothes and sunscreen)	(knife: plus a gear repair kit)
a mirror	(navigation: map, compass, altimeter, GPS device, or satellite messenger)	(first aid kit)	extra flip-flops	entertainment like video games or books

Backcountry- a remote undeveloped rural area.

Badlands Word Search

1. badland
2. bison
3. erosion
4. south dakota
5. prairie dog
6. fossil
7. lakota
8. sunset
9. pronghorn
10. grasslands
11. sage creek
12. hiking
13. ferret
14. rattlesnake
15. stargazing
16. sunrise
17. butte
18. bighorn

```
S W B I G H O R N S K L F W K
N O S I B I L E S H E O W R J
T E U R K A O R C C S B A P B
S M P T E R R E F S R L U U R
C E A I H H I K I N G U T K A
A O L D Y D S L D B T T A C T
R O A D P R A I R I E D O G T
P S B S S E G K G W E I R X L
R T H S U E R O S I O N P E
E A I C N N C Y H T N G O R S
Q R A H S C R C N N A E N O N
S G N I E M E I S M O K I N A
L A K O T A E S S J R A Q G K
J Z G T L E K E S E O R V H E
N I X A K B A D L A N D H O M
X N T F A R E G L Z E S Q R E
U G R A S S L A N D S P V N B
C J D O S R E D N Y M A L A S
```

Answers: Find the Match!
What are Baby Animals Called?

Match the animal to its baby. The first one is done for you.

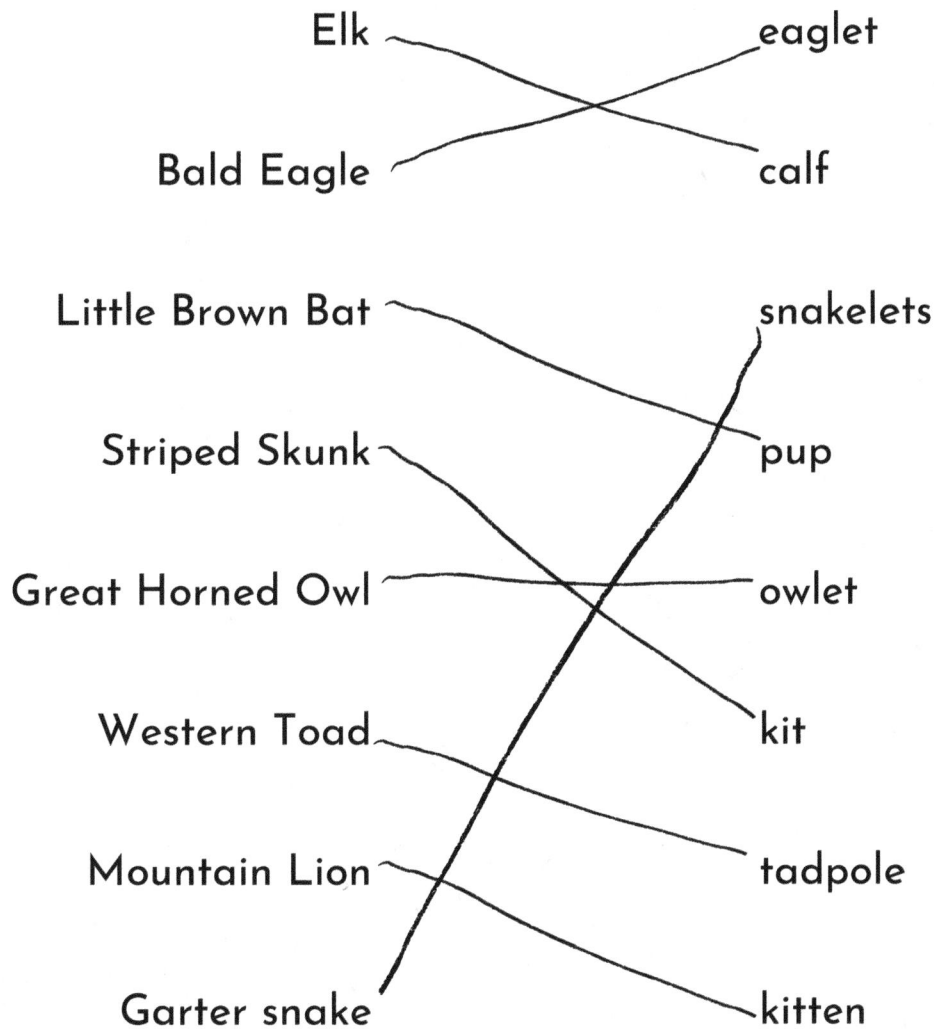

Elk — eaglet

Bald Eagle — calf

Little Brown Bat — snakelets

Striped Skunk — pup

Great Horned Owl — owlet

Western Toad — kit

Mountain Lion — tadpole

Garter snake — kitten

Solution: Hike the Fossil Exhibit Trail

The Geologic Formations of the Badlands

The formations in Badlands National Park and badlands formations around the world are the end-product of two simple processes: **deposition** and **erosion**. Deposition is the process of rocks gradually building up. Erosion is the process of rocks gradually wearing away. These rocks have much to teach us about Earth's history.

1. sandstone
2. siltstone
3. volcanic ash
4. butte
5. shale
6. canyon
7. ridge
8. Yellow Mounds
9. Chandron
10. Brule
11. Sharps
12. Rockyford Ash
13. erosion
14. deposition
15. eruption
16. fossils
17. Big Pig Dig
18. river

L E R O S I O N H B D N O W S
H A D A A I A Z S I E O W R H
T V D N N I T T A G A I K O A
C H A N D R O N C P U T B C R
C F N A S H A L E I Y I S K P
M O D V T R R K C G A S I Y S
C S S E O R C E R D O O L F N
A S B E N L I R D I L P V O B
L I H O E I C O E G U E E R N
L L I R S M O A K E U D U D O
I S I L T S T O N E K L N A I
S C N S K A O I S I E K T S T
T A O S F H I N Z I C L W H P
E N R E L I V E I B D A V E U
R Y E L L O W M O U N D S E R
T O V L G R E E N T A K E H E
U N I E S A E N N T A P V E B
C J R I D G E E R E Y S I O N

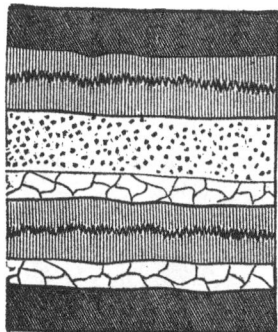

Answers: Leave No Trace Quiz

Leave No Trace is a concept that helps people make decisions during outdoor recreation that protects the environment. There are seven principles that guide us when we spend time outdoors, whether you are in a national park or not. Are you an expert in Leave No Trace? Take this quiz and find out!

1. How can you plan ahead and prepare to ensure you have the best experience you can in the National Park?

    A. Make sure you stop by the ranger station for a map and to ask about current conditions.

2. What is an example of traveling on a durable surface?

    A. Walking only on the designated path.

3. Why should you dispose of waste properly?

    C. So that other peoples' experiences of the park are not impacted by you leaving your waste behind.

4. How can you best follow the concept "leave what you find"?

    B. Take pictures but leave any physical items where they are.

5. What is not a good example of minimizing campfire impacts?

    C. Building a new campfire ring in a location that has a better view.

6. What is a poor example of respecting wildlife?

    A. Building squirrel houses out of rocks from the river so the squirrels have a place to live.

7. How can you show consideration of other visitors?

    B. Wear headphones on the trail if you choose to listen to music.

Solution: Spot the Wildlife at Robert's Prairie Dog Town!

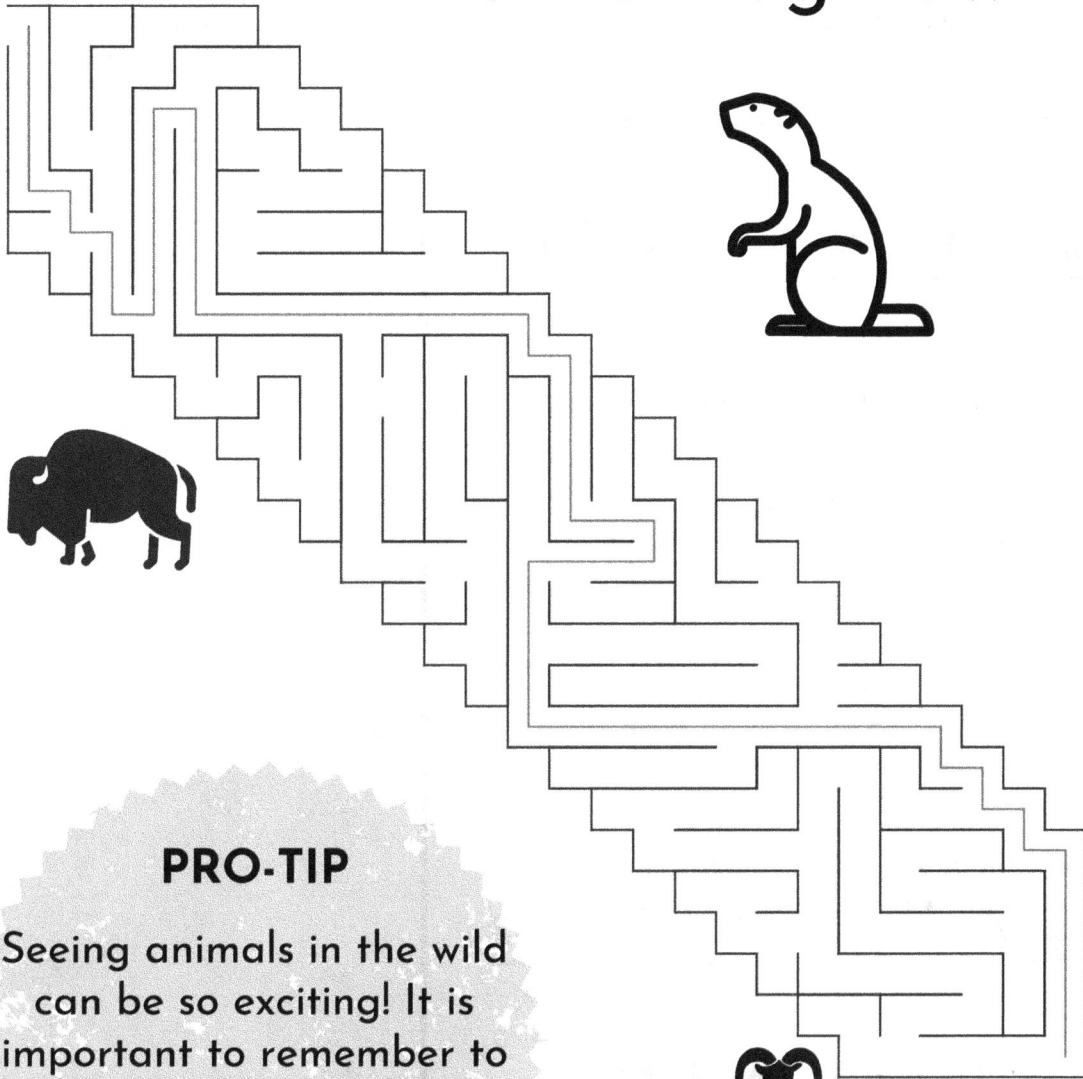

PRO-TIP

Seeing animals in the wild can be so exciting! It is important to remember to keep a minimum of 100 yards between you any wildlife you see.

Decoding Using American Sign Language

American Sign Language, also called ASL for short, is a language that many Deaf people or people who are hard of hearing use to communicate. People use ASL to communicate with their hands. Did you know people from all over the country and world travel to national parks? You may hear people speaking other languages. You might also see people using ASL. Use the American Manual Alphabet chart to decode some national parks facts.

This was the first national park to be established:

Y E L L O W S T O N E

This is the biggest national park in the US:

W R A N G E L L -

S T . E L I A S

This is the most visited national park:

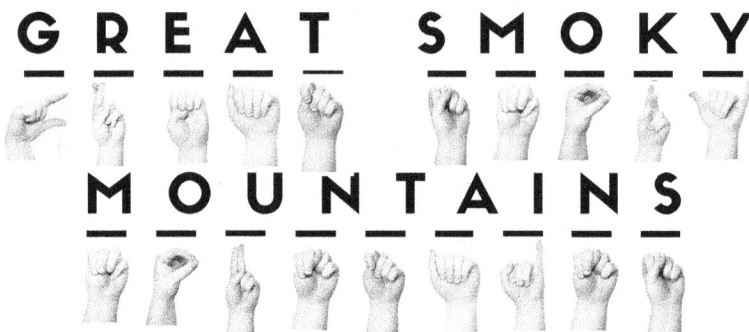

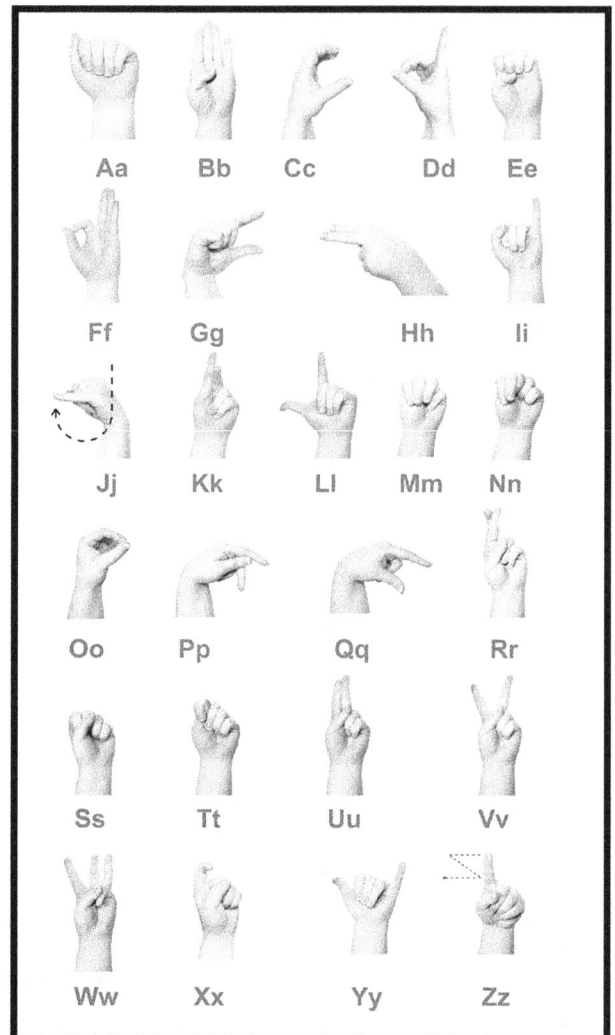

G R E A T   S M O K Y

M O U N T A I N S

Aa	Bb	Cc	Dd	Ee
Ff	Gg		Hh	Ii
Jj	Kk	Ll	Mm	Nn
Oo	Pp		Qq	Rr
Ss	Tt		Uu	Vv
Ww	Xx		Yy	Zz

Hint: Pay close attention to the position of the thumb!

Try it! Using the chart, try to make the letters of the alphabet with your hand. What is the hardest letter to make? Can you spell out your name? Show a friend or family member and have them watch you spell out the name of the national park you are in.

Go Horseback Riding at Sage Creek Campground

Help find the horse's lost shoe!

start here →

DID YOU KNOW?

There are no marked trails for horseback riding, allowing for horse owners to explore all 64,000 acres of the Badlands Wilderness Area!

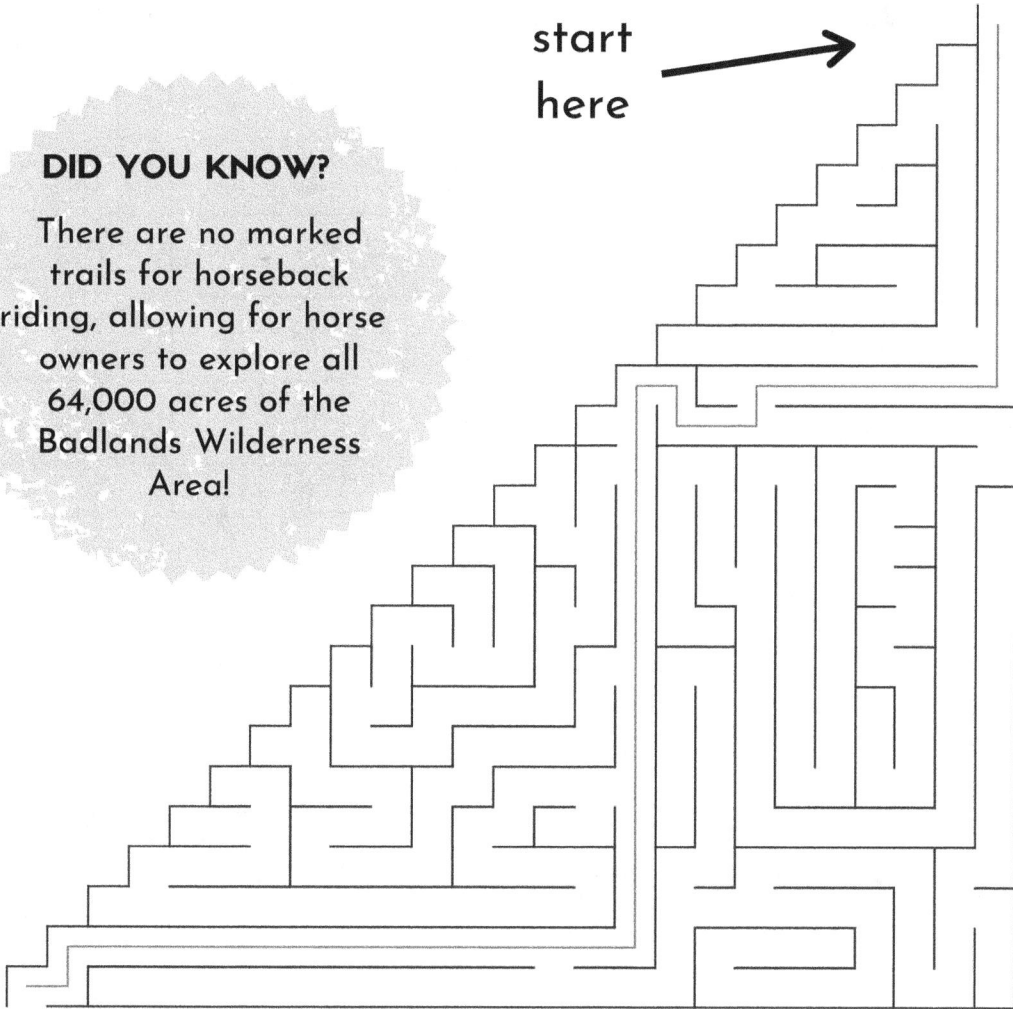

Let's Go Camping
Word Search

1. tent
2. camp stove
3. sleeping bag
4. bug spray
5. sunscreen
6. map
7. flashlight
8. pillow
9. lantern
10. ice
11. snacks
12. smores
13. water
14. first aid kit
15. chair
16. cards
17. books
18. games
19. trail
20. hat

```
D P P I L L O W D B T E A C I
E O A D P R E A A M B R C A N
P W C A M P S T O V E I H X G
R A H S G E L E B E E D A P S
E L B U G S P R A Y N G I E A
S I A H G C I C N N M E R C N
C W N L A F I R S K O O B F K
M T A E M I L E L H M R W L J
T A P R E A O R E S L B A A B
S M P A S R R T E N T L U S C
C E A I I R C G P E I U J H A
S S N A C K S S I M O K I L R
I J R S F O I S N J R A Q I D
C Y E T L E V E G U O R V G S
E W T A K C A B B S S O H H M
X J N F I R S T A I D K I T T
U A A E S S E N G E T P V A B
C J L I A R T D N A M A H A S
```

68

Fish at the Badlands

1.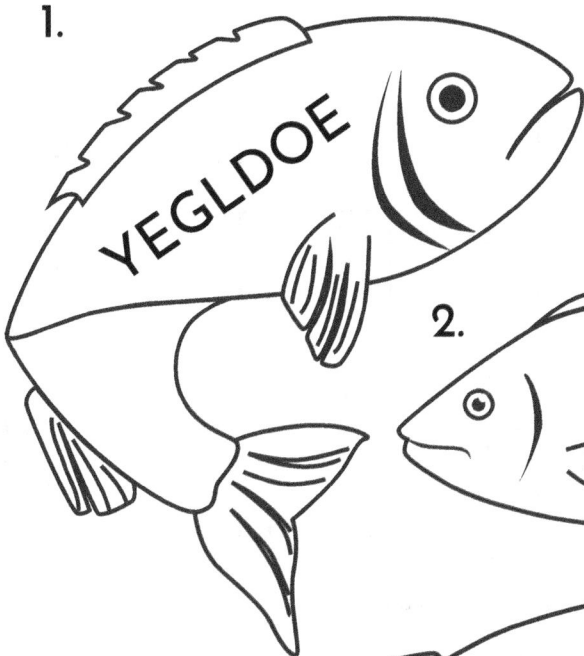

2.

Unscramble these common fish names that live in the park.

3.

4.

5.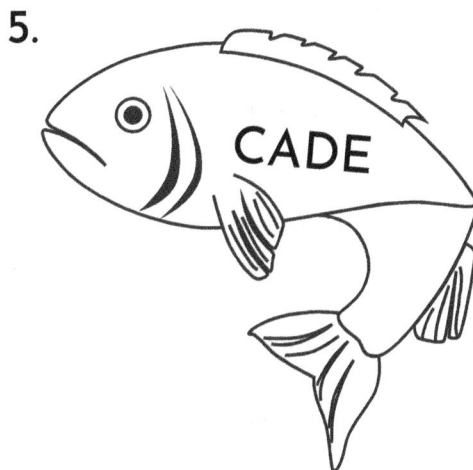

1. GOLDEYE
2. CARP
3. MINNOW
4. BULLHEAD
5. DACE

Word Bank

carp
shiner
goldeye
minnow
bullhead
sauger
redhorse
dace

Answers: Other National Parks

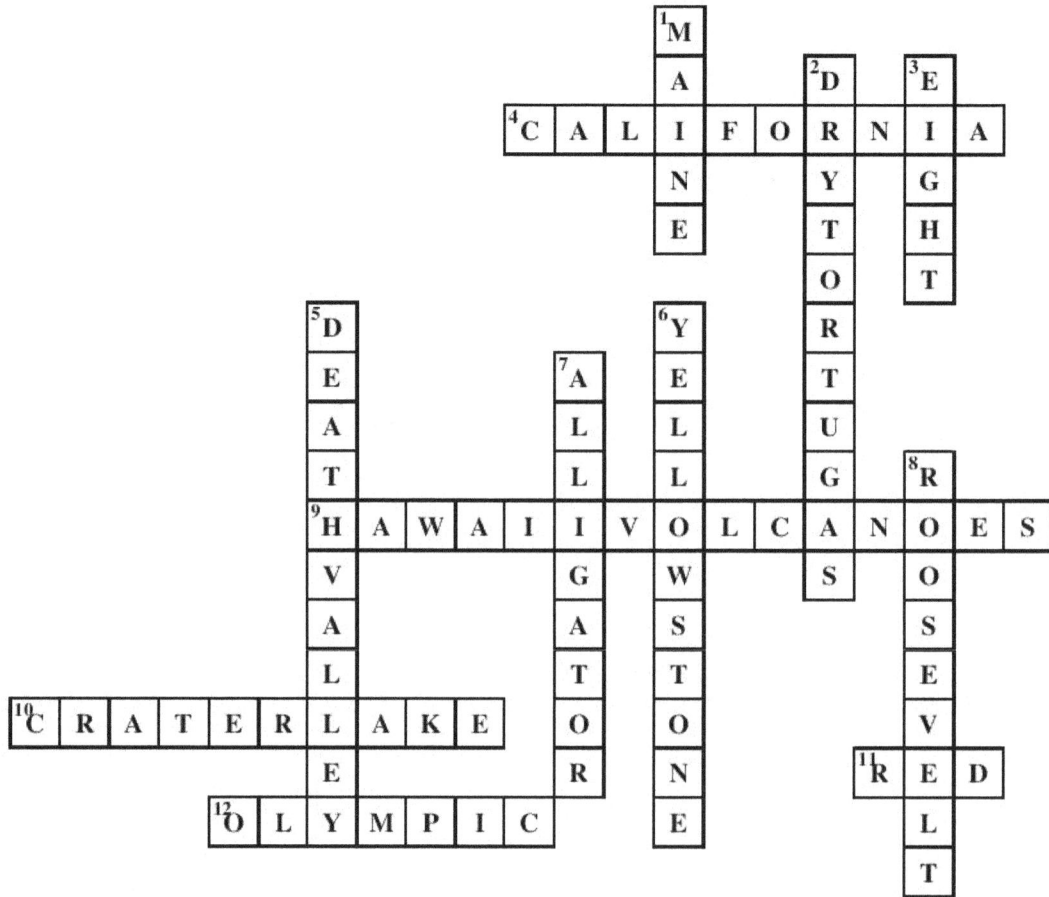

The completed crossword grid contains the following answers:

- 1 Down: MAINE
- 2 Down: DRYTORTUGAS
- 3 Down: EIGHT
- 4 Across: CALIFORNIA
- 5 Down: DEATHVALLEY
- 6 Down: YELLOWSTONE
- 7 Down: ALLIGATOR
- 8 Down: ROOSEVELT
- 9 Across: HAWAIIVOLCANOES
- 10 Across: CRATERLAKE
- 11 Across: RED
- 12 Across: OLYMPIC

Down

1. State where Acadia National Park is located
2. This National Park has the Spanish word for turtle in it
3. Number of National Parks in Alaska
5. This National Park has some of the hottest temperatures in the world
6. This National Park is the only one in Idaho
7. This toothsome creature can be famously found in Everglades National Park
8. Only president with a national park named for them

Across

4. This state has the most National Parks
9. This park has some of the newest land in the US, caused by a volcanic eruption
10. This park has the deepest lake in the United States
11. This color shows up in the name of a National Park in California
12. This National Park deserves a gold medal

Answers: Where National Park Will You Go Next?

1. Zion
2. Big Bend
3. Glacier
4. Olympic
5. Sequoia
6. Bryce
7. Mesa Verde
8. Biscayne
9. Wind Cave
10. Great Basin
11. Katmai
12. Yellowstone
13. Voyageurs
14. Arches
15. Badlands
16. Denali
17. Glacier Bay
18. Hot Springs

```
F M M E S A V E R D E B N E Y
E A B I G B E N D E S A S E M
Y L I C A L O Y N E E D L T G
D M G A S S A U C N R L U E R
C E L I I T S C R E O A A K E
S N A W Y E E O I W T N A C A
G I C H A A Q C S E M D N S T
N O I Z P R U T I M R S N E B
I W E L M P O N B W E B K H A
R J R F D N I F L I H B U C S
P A B E E S A N E S O P W R I
S J A E N Y A C S I B A U A N
T C Y I A D O H H Y M E A L R
O T A T L M L E S E G R W R J
H S T O I K A T M A I R O P B
I C H U R C O L Y M P I C O U
O Y G T S D E O S B R Y C E T
W I N D C A V E I N R O H E M
```

LITTLE BISON

Press

Little Bison Press is an independent children's book publisher based in the Pacific Northwest. We promote exploration, conservation, and adventure through our books. Established in 2021, our passion for outside spaces and travel inspired the creation of Little Bison Press.

We seek to publish books that support children in learning about and caring for the natural places in our world.

To learn more, visit:
LittleBisonPress.com

Want more free games and activities? Visit our website!